1   A Highland 'clachan' or settlement, at Loch Duich, Wester Ross; *c.*1880

Victorian and Edwardian

HIGHLANDS

from old photographs

FRANCIS THOMPSON

B. T. BATSFORD LTD
LONDON

To the Highland folk of yesteryear

Lichen
clings fast to these stones
like dried tears.
Once
they articulated
in a community of functional interest
to shelter
against wind and rain.
They absorbed,
with an infinite sympathy,
the quiet sounds
of the household.

Now,
after the searing heat of their firing,
and the harshness of their breaking,
embedded for ever
in a stony memory,
they lie
sunk in a sea of bracken,
silent in a wash of green.
Only the wind here
tries
to make amends.

FRANCIS THOMPSON

First published 1976
Text copyright Francis Thompson 1976

Filmset by Servis Filmsetting Ltd, Manchester
Printed in Great Britain by The Anchor Press Ltd, Tiptree
for the Publishers B.T. Batsford Ltd,
4 Fitzhardinge Street, London W1H 0AH
ISBN 0 7134 3224 1

CONTENTS

PAGE

Acknowledgments   6

Introduction   7

ILLUSTRATION NUMBER

People and Characters   7–33

Highland Homes   34–57

People at Work – *Domestic and Community Occupations*   58–74

People at Work – *The Land*   75–85

People at Work – *The Sea*   86–96

Events and Occasions   97–109

Getting About   110–125

Sport and Pleasure   126–132

Industry   133–137

ACKNOWLEDGMENTS

In a book of this kind the real credit must go to those who made these photographs available, or who, by realising their worth, made some active attempt to preserve old records. Thus, the following, though a mere list of names, are due the thanks of readers who might find the collection adding to their knowledge, appreciation and sympathy for long-past times in the region. The list, however, and this must be stressed, merely manifests the real help, often at the expense of time and energy, which the author received. In a number of cases contact with one source of pictures led to another source, or led to individuals who gave invaluable help in dating photographs which were doubtful as to their date or place. Two sources of photographs merit special mention: the West Highland Museum and the Tain Museum. Both have excellent collections crying out for expert attention in mounting and preservation, but, because they are small and local, lack the funds necessary to effect the work required. Much of great interest is perforce resting in boxes, unseen by visitors to the Museums; the situation does need the attention of those who are now responsible for regional archives and who, it is hoped, are aware that books and artifacts are but only one facet of regional life in the past. My particular thanks are due to Mr Hamish Campbell, Edinburgh, who, often at some inconvenience and discomfort, copied and printed the original photographs, some quite faded and thought beyond reproduction.

The Staff of the *Oban Times*, Oban
The Staff of the *Highland News*, Inverness
Mr A. Johnston, Photographer, Wick
The Staff of Aberdeen Public Library
The Staff of Edinburgh Public Library
The Staff of the Country Life Archives, Edinburgh
Miss Sally Archibald, Curator, West Highland Museum, Fort William
Mrs Rosemary MacKenzie, Tain Museum, Tain
Mrs Anne Gordon, Nigg, Tain, Easter Ross

Mr A. M. Morrison, District Librarian, Stornoway
Mrs Cathcart, Inverness
Mr A. Fraser, Bishopton, Glasgow
Mr Ken Humphreys, Dingwall
The Misses Munro, Inverness
Dr I. F. Grant, Edinburgh
Wm. Sanderson & Son Limited, South Queensferry
The British Aluminium Company, London
Mr T. B. MacAulay, Stornoway

INTRODUCTION

When Queen Victoria took her seat upon the throne, the occasion did not mark the beginning of happy times in the Highlands and Islands of Scotland. Far from it; her reign saw nothing but conditions of life in which none but the toughest and strongest-willed survived. The folk lived through their hard times with a bravery that we, this century, might not understand. There was, in fact, a sheer will to live, derived from an inherited streak of stubbornness left over from previous generations who also had to make do with what they had – or die. On the other side of the social coin, however, those with ample means enjoyed a lifestyle which was acted out in a world as remote, strange and different from that of the poor Highland folk as could be imagined. The twain met but at a discreet distance: contacts were rather through agents such as estate factors and the two societies might well have existed in different ages. Thus, the Highlands and Islands of Scotland were at once the pride of possession of the aristocracy, many alien to the region, the old Highland chiefs and lairds having gone, sold out, or had their estates in the hands of the tallyman; at the same time the region was the very foothold on life for a vast number of people, many of whom had as much legal right to the land on which they lived as had a fruit fly on an apple. Even the centres of urban ostentation, towns like Inverness, Wick and Dingwall, were no more than inconvenient jumbles of houses and shops: places where people found work which was no easier, and a lot less satisfactory, than had they stayed in the countryside, on familiar subsistence levels certainly but at least living in their natural communities.

The rhythms of the lifestyles in the Highlands and Islands were Gaelic-based, as they still are though now somewhat diluted. During the period from 1881 onwards, the ten-yearly census of Scotland had sought information as to the ability to speak Gaelic amongst the population aged three years and over. In 1881, 231,594 persons claimed 'habitually' to speak Gaelic (out of a Scottish population of 3,425,151 aged three years and over). In 1891, 254,415 (out of 3,721,778) were Gaelic-speaking. In the context of the Highlands and Islands, this figure represents almost 90% of the population, with the notable exception of Caithness. The Gaelic line extended from the Western Isles to a line roughly drawn from Caithness (on its Sutherland marches) down to south Perthshire and across to the Mull of Kintyre – an area representing about 60% of Scotland's total land area. There was thus a significant cultural and linguistic difference between the Highlands and Islands and the rest of Scotland, which has since been so diluted that at the present time only 90,000 people profess to speak and read Gaelic. The dilution was mainly the direct result of the mass emigration of Highland folk to the south (Glasgow in particular) and overseas. However, despite the predominance of Gaelic as the lingua franca of Highland communities, tourists and travellers were able to get about in the region without difficulty – English was also spoken and understood. Indeed, Gaelic was one of the attractions when visiting the region because it provided a 'foreign atmosphere' which was lacking elsewhere in Scotland.

Yet another important aspect of the region to be noted and understood is that industry as such was largely absent during the reigns of Victoria and Edward VII; though there were pockets of small industrial operations. Life was rather thirled to activities associated with land use and, in the coastal areas, with the fishing industry which, by the late nineteenth century, was assuming boom proportions. Highland folk were, however, merely employees on both land and sea. The result was that the cash generated went outside the region and hardly benefited the communities which so badly needed improved social services such as good roads, hospitals and schools.

Bad things still happened in the Highlands: atrocities were committed in the name of landlords (usually absent from the scene of the crime) which were centred round the need to clear people off land to create vast sheep runs and deer forests. Only in 1886 did the Highland crofter become a legal entity, recognised by the Statute Book as being entitled by right to security of tenure through the Crofters Act; though the Act failed to provide the most important need: encouragement to improve land use methods. The Act was one of fossilisation with the results which one sees today in the Highlands: desolation and acres upon acres of derelict land that once supported a significant population of both people and cattle.

During the reigns of both monarchs the region was in a kind of cocoon, both insulated and isolated from the spectrum of industrial and commercial activity which existed in other parts of the British Isles. This narrower horizon is reflected in the photographs in this book, which, while panoramic to a degree, lacks range of incident and interest.

To give one instance: the years of the 1880s saw agitation in the Highlands and Islands. Land, its possession and its use, was the issue at stake and violence was the order of the day. The inevitable course of law, made by and favoured towards land-owning interests, resulted in opposition in many parts of the region which produced acts of extreme cruelty and violence, particularly on the island of Skye. Yet, except in drawings subsequently reproduced as etchings in newspapers, we have no photographs of the wild and bloody scenes on Skye, depicting, say, the Battle of the Braes.

There was, however, one recording angel: George Washington Wilson, of Aberdeen: had it not been for his roving camera, much of the life of the region would be visually

3 Croft houses near Stornoway, Lewis; 1890

unknown today. As Photographer Royal for Scotland he used some 20 years of his life and that of his staff (from 1866 to 1886) travelling about the British Isles, and occasionally to Europe, to take some 25,000 pictures of buildings, scenes and people and their environments. Most of the photographs were printed by daylight on albumenised paper, sensitised by Mr Wilson with nitrate of silver, toned with chloride of gold and fixed with hypo-sulphate of soda. As a contribution to the visual record of life in the Highlands and Islands of Scotland, Wilson's is magnificent and we would be the less informed were it not for his dogged intent and interest in his work. Though one might have wished that many of those Highland tourists with both literary ambition and ability had left better records of conditions in the region particularly in the decades after the Crofters Act of 1886 – and had been aware of the fact that photographic records would have enhanced their written observations. As it is, only one photographer in the 1880s, whose true identity can only be guessed, has left us with a small collection of surpassing interest but frustrating in its paucity. That photographic record of some evictions in North Uist about 1890 is rare and only serves to underline the dearth of similar records which might have been taken of other incidents in the region.

Thus it is that the present collection of photographs has its limitations and in no way can it be said of it that it is wholly representative. Even so, the final selection of what has been uncovered in both institutional archives and in private collections does touch on most aspects of the region and takes in the activities of both the commonalty and *les riches*.

The accurate dating of a number of photographs has proved difficult; however, research among written records has yielded sufficient information for dating and so the dates attributed to the pictures are within two or three years. One particular problem in dating was due to the fact that often fashions were in use in the region long after they had become archaic in other parts of the British Isles; a traditional mode of dress often lasted for half a generation – indeed, the older the person the more were the styles retained to be half a century out of date.

Many of the photographers are unknown, save for a record of their names, with one or two outstanding exceptions. Apart from George Washington Wilson, a number of pictures were taken by identifiable people, such as William Smith, of Tain, of whom we include a fine self-portrait. It is suspected with reasonable grounds that some of the photographs of scenes in the Hebrides (eg, the evictions and Benbecula Fair Day) were taken by Mrs Amy Goodrich-Freer, a lady of mixed abilities and fixed mind and intentions who created some controversy in the fields of Highland folklore and psychic research at the turn of the century. Her pictures, originally on glass plates, were discovered by chance a few years ago and saved from destruction for posterity.

During the search for photographs, many names of photographers cropped up; their main interest being in portraiture, they did not contribute to the visual interpretation of the Highland scene. Among the popular names in the Highlands were John Collier, Inverness, described as a 'Photographic Artist'. Mr A. Johnston, of Wick, operated from 'The North of Scotland Photographic Rooms', as his son still does today. John Munro of Dingwall was also pleased to describe himself as a photographic artist and advertised: 'Enlargements on any size of paper or Canvas artistically finished in Oil, Water Colours or Crayon, can at any time be produced without another sitting'. J. MacMahon had studios in both Inverness and Strathpeffer, the latter being the popular Victorian watering place with a reputation which rivalled that of English Bath. The studio of D. Whyte, Inverness, advertised the work of the then 'Artist and Photographer', which business still survives.

Last, but by no means least, was William Smith of Tain, 'Patronised by H. M. the Queen and the Royal Family'. Smith was an unusual man and, from his activities and interests, it is no wonder he attracted royal attention. In his lifetime he was Vice-Chairman of the Tain Liberal Association and founded the Tain Ragged School in 1858. As a photographer he was much in demand and once sent to Mr Gladstone some Christmas and Birthday cards containing pictures of Mr Gladstone surrounded by all the Ministers of his Cabinet. Smith also photographed Queen Victoria, Princess

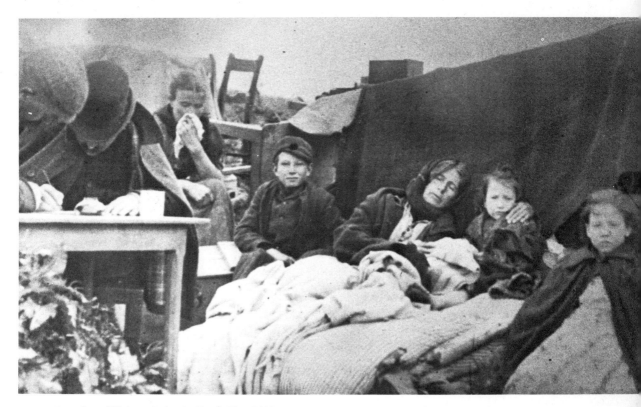

4   Out into the cold! An eviction in North Uist, 1895

Beatrice, Prince Leopold and the Duchess of Sutherland, with the tenacious John Brown in attendance. In 1855 Smith advertised: 'William Smith, Bookseller, Tain, respectfully announces that he is now in a position to take photographs on Cobdianised Glass and, having erected a Glass-House for the purpose, they can be taken during any state of the weather'.

5 William Smith,
photographer, Tain. A
self-portrait taken *c*.1870

6   Tweed cloth from St Kilda was a best-seller last century. The photograph shows some of the finished product being baled for shipment to Oban and to London's fashion houses; 1886

PEOPLE AND CHARACTERS

Any community living close to its origins, and recognising in these the bases for the peculiar rhythms in the lifestyles of its members, must perforce produce a number of individuals of strong character who, in their own way, and however idiosyncratic, represent the bulk of the rest. Some of these characters are here presented, along with representatives from the majority who opted for the quiet life and conformation to society's norms. They are all, however, the natural products of an environment which was harsh and demanded both physical strength and spiritual tenacity for the continuity of life.

There are indications of ethnic origins, Celtic and Norse; though it must be stressed that only in certain parts of the region do the physical Norse characteristics predominate. For the most part these folk are Celtic, Gaelic-speaking and display distinct racial traits. Perhaps some faces show traces of refinement, particularly on the eastern seaboard of the Highlands, which might be expected in districts where there was a free mixing of people with Flemish origins (say from the north-east coastal areas around Buckie in Banffshire) marrying and intermarrying with folk of the eastern Highland seaboard of Caithness, Sutherland and Easter Ross.

Farther west the mixing was less frequent; marriages tended to take place within distinct communities or within a specific area of communities and so racial strains were retained with a degree of purity. In this context, and of particular interest, are the faces of the St Kildans, the product of a community which satisfied its need for continuity from its own internal elements. Though one must stress that when we look at the St Kildans we also see Hebrideans, for the original St Kildan community was virtually wiped out as the result of disease, epidemics and massacre and so had to be restocked. Even so, the faces represent the last but one generation of true St Kilda folk (the island was deserted in 1930).

The Highlanders are here photographed as they go about their business, their work, and, seldom, their play. One cries out for a sight of the folk intent on enjoying life, as they invariably could, if one is to believe the observations of travellers in the High-

7   A character from Tarfside, Glenusk, beside a 'muckle wheel' spinning wheel; 1900

8   A pause during a discussion by members of the St Kilda Parliament; c.1880

lands. As it is, we are presented with set studies and character pieces of 'still life' which are a far cry from the vibrant people the Highlanders are at heart.

Even so, one is grateful for those who saw photography as an outlet for their creative instincts and provided not only a form of art but a permanent record of their generation, fixed in the perpetuity of hypo-sulphate of soda.

It is useful to reflect that the people in this photographic gallery were, for the most part, the last representatives of a generation which was almost wholly Gaelic-speaking, with a modest facility in the English language. They were unconscious tradition-bearers for a culture of more than a thousand years standing and were in fact, though they did not know it, living in a time when the strong ropes that had bound them to the past were beginning to fray into the mere threads that they are today.

They had an unexpected advocate, however: Queen Victoria, who insisted that Highland children should be educated through the medium of their own language. In 1849 she communicated her ideas to Lord Lansdowne, one of her Ministers: '. . . it is really a great mistake that the people should be constantly talking a language which they often cannot read and generally not write'. In his reply, Lord Lansdowne undertook '. . . to combine instruction in the Gaelic with the English language . . . and to have a view to it in the choice of inspectors'. Victoria even had her *Highland Journal* translated into Gaelic. It may well have been, however, that her interest in Gaelic was too strongly underlined by 'Balmorality' and its attendant John Brown, dancing his sinuous way into the Queen's affections, for her opinions and desires for the Gaelic language to be taken seriously. In the event, the Education (Scotland) Act of 1872 completely ignored the fact that nearly a quarter of a million Highland subjects spoke the language and used it as a means of communication for more than domestic purposes.

The land-owning class in the Highlands has its representatives here. They are, of course, in the numerical minority, though their influence affected the daily lives of thousands. However, they deserve a place in the Highland gallery because they are a part of the later decades of regional history. Some members of this class are despised to this very day; others are remembered with affection because of their interest and concern for the lot of their tenants. Of many lairds it was said: 'He did us no harm, but he also did us no good'.

The young Earl of Dunmore, of the estate in North Harris, had cause to be satisfied, if not proud, of the fact that his family had the initiative and commercial awareness of the possibilities of a local cloth woven in Harris. Within a few short years, the London fashion houses were crying out for ever-increasing quantities of Harris Tweed and so, by their demand, created the foundations for the present-day, multi-million pound (sterling) industry. Sadly, families such as the Dunmores were the exception rather

9 Women of St Kilda; *c.* 1880

than the rule – but the story of a local cloth making good in the wide world outside the Highlands and Islands of Scotland is a fair note of happy tenor on which to introduce the reader to the folk of the Highlands.

10   Aristocracy in the Highlands: the group includes Anne, Countess of Cromarty, and the Princess of Wales. Taken at Foulis Castle, 1866

12   A group of employees from a cycle shop, Tain, 1900. Note the street water hydrant

13   A group photograph, possibly composite, from Caithness; *c.*1870

15 In Fishertown, Cromarty,
Easter Ross; *c*.1880

16 Men of Tain (taken by the Scottish Photographic Touring & Pictorial Post Card Company,
Glasgow); *c*.1890

17 On the island of St Kilda; c.1890

18 Community gossip on the island of St Kilda; c.1890

19 Two octogenarians from Skye; c.1880

20 Beer drinkers of Wick;
*c.*1890

21 St Kilda women and girls;
*c.*1880

22 Fisher girls at Cromarty, Easter Ross; *c.*1905

23 Ladies of Fortrose, Black Isle, Easter Ross; 1880

24 Prim, neat and tidy Mrs
Gilmour, a 'big-house'
governess; 1880

26 'Bright young things' on
North Uist; *c.*1900

25 Schoolchildren on St Kilda; 1890

27 Bait carrier from Easter Ross; c.1890

28 'Rory Toe', the Town Crier of Tain and a familiar street newsvendor. He earned his nickname from his large, outsize feet; Tain, 1890

30 *Right* 'Rabbity Tam', a poacher from Sutherland; otherwise known as John MacKenzie; *c.*1880. This portrait is by William Smith, Tain

29 A Highland hermit at Calrossie Woods, near Tain. In his youth Davy Gogie saw a murder being committed; the incident so unnerved him that he dropped out of society to lead his lonely life; *c.*1900

31a

31a–d From a Highland
family album; *c*.1880

31c

31b

31d

32   From a Highland family album; 'The play's the thing!'; c.1880

33   Sir Kenneth and Lady MacKenzie

34   Ben More; in the foreground, Glendochart; *c*.1875

HIGHLAND HOMES

Homes in the Highlands and Islands last century ranged from mere hovels and shake-downs to palatial residences. Highland settlements also revealed the same spectrum: from clusters of cluttered thatched houses, with orderly planning hardly in evidence, to well-laid out streets of towns and large villages.

Perhaps the most interesting types of Highland homes were those which evolved by necessity rather than by design and which showed the ability of the common folk to devise dwellings to protect themselves from a rigorous climate, and that with the minimum of suitable building materials. Houses were functional shelters from inclement weather; in good weather it was normal to live outdoors. Furniture too was functional, and its design was based on the provision of the minimum of comfort. Generally, these one-storey, stone-walled thatched houses represent the folk-architecture of the old Highlands before they were finally superseded by the dictates of new fashion and Local Authority health regulations.

Essentially, then, the old Highland house was that of the outdoor man; however, the significance of the expression *aig an teine* (at the fire) applied to the main apartment of the building at once suggests the value he attached to the social graces and aspirations of friendship. The house was planned to provide shelter from cold, wind, and rain, with the warmth of social converse engendered by the comforting glow of the peat fire. Boswell, describing his stay at Coirechatachan, remarked: '. . . we had no rooms that we could command, for the good people here had no notion that a man could have any occasion but for a mere sleeping place'.

The popular name for these simple dwellings was, and is, the 'black house' – the origin of the name is confused, rising from a phonetic similarity between the word *dubh* (black) and *tugadh* (thatch) – and they were to be found from the Hebrides to Perthshire. There were local variations in the general design, reflecting the resources of building materials available. In the treeless Hebrides, wood had to be searched for on the shores, cast up after storms. On the mainland, wood was plentiful from the forest, a fact which was also reflected in better house furnishings.

The following is a description of a general nature of a mid-Victorian black house: 'In the Outer Isles the walls of the houses are very thick, varying from four to eight

35   A croft house ('black house') at Kilmuir, Skye; 1880

feet. A facing of stone is to the inside and another to the outside, the space between being filled with stones, gravel or earth. The corners of the building are rounded, and there are no gables, the low walls being level right round. The roof is raised from the inner facing of the wall, the rest being laid over with turf and green grass where pet sheep or lambs often graze and occasionally – when the building abuts on a bank, as is sometimes the case – a courageous cow and calf or even a mare and foal. Two or three stone steps project from the wall near the door, to enable the family to ascend and descend when occasion requires. In suitable summer weather the women of the family take possession of these grassy wall-tops and sew, spin or knit and look about them, while the household dogs sleep beside them in the sun. The principal object of these stone steps, however, is to enable the men to get up to thatch and rope the house, ladders being short, rare or non-existent.'

The thatch was made from bent grass, heather, barley straw or rushes, depending on what was available locally. In some districts the roof was regarded as a moveable item; the tenant would provide his own roof timbers, the walls belonging to the tacksman or laird: 'His capital consists of his cattle, his sheep . . . the rafters of his house'.

The fire was in the middle of the floor to allow maximum radiation of heat and to benefit all the household. Doors were crude and never locked. The key of a door was associated with meanness and that cardinal sin: inhospitality – *cho mosach ris a' ghlais*, as mean as the lock, is a well-used proverb indicating the attitude of mind of the Highlander to the moral obligation of welcoming the stranger at his door. If privacy were required, a stick was fixed athwart the door and removed as soon as circumstances permitted. Furniture consisted of simple benches, stools, box beds and a table or trestle. Most of these were home-made. Light was provided by a simple *cruisgean*, a dish of oil with a wick of cloth rag or dried pith of rushes.

In old Celtic society, towns were the exception rather than the rule, an aspect of culture which still obtained in Victorian and Edwardian times, when the largest burgh in the Highlands was Inverness, far ahead of other urban growths such as Dingwall, Oban, Stornoway, Fort William and Thurso, where the population was numbered in a paltry thousand or two inhabitants. These towns followed their noses for their planning, displaying an empirical attitude to housing, streets and amenities, which

36   A crofter's house at Loch Ewe, Wester Ross; 1889

37   By the ingle-nook; *c.*1900

resulted in today's luxurious atmosphere of 'quaintness' in some quarters. Town dwellings were largely just as functional as their country counterparts.

The rural equivalent of the urban settlement was the crofting township, whose history goes back to those dreadful years of the Clearances, when people were forced into unsuitable and often alien areas to recover, as best they could, from the new impositions on life of which dispossession, refugee status and starvation were but a few. Many townships grew from the urgent need for the dispossessed to rehouse themselves almost entirely out of their own resources. That these townships survived and developed to become recognisable communities is a tribute to the tenacity of many of those who are photographed here. It is this which must be borne in mind when one views these pictures, comparing the resplendent interiors of the houses of the privileged classes with the often depressing and degrading conditions of those who had nothing.

38 A tinker's camp in the Highlands; *c*.1885

39 Crofting houses on Skye, 1880

40 A homestead on South Uist, 1886. Note the peat-clad walls

41 A croft house in Wester Ross, 1880. A barrel has been pressed into service as a chimney

42 A kelp-maker's hut on South Uist, 1880

43 The house merges into the environment on Barra, 1880

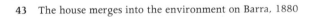

44 The photographer called this hut on South Uist 'a poor house'; 1880

45 The last of the black houses in Fort Augustus, Inverness-shire; 1880

47 On Barra; 1880

48 Housing at Kildonan,
Sutherland; 1880

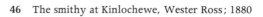

46　The smithy at Kinlochewe, Wester Ross; 1880

49　Neat housing at Glen Orchy; 1900

50 Fincastle, at Amhuinnsuidhe, Isle of Harris, under construction; built by Lord Dunmore. Lady Dunmore started off the now famous Harris Tweed industry. Now called Amhuinnsuidhe Castle, it was here that J. M. Barrie wrote his *Mary Rose*; 1866

51 Knockrobbie, near Kirkhill, Inverness-shire, 1900. An old description of the house says: 'It was from this mansion the Laird of Reelig oppressed the poor. I can still remember the bucket placed in the kitchen to catch the damp through the roof. The house is no longer standing'

52 Cawdor Castle, near Nairn: the mantelpiece in the Blue Room;
1880

53   Balmoral Castle: Queen Victoria's dressing room; 1880

54 Cromwell Street, Stornoway, Lewis; 1890

55 Main Street, Tobermoray, Isle of Mull; 1880

56 Station Square, Inverness; 1890

57 High Street, Inverness; 1890

PEOPLE AT WORK
Domestic and Community Occupations

Life in the rural areas of the Highlands and Islands during the reigns of Victoria and Edward was one of continual movement in order to make the work of each day, save the Sabbath, a significant element in the final aggregate of a season. Work was done in two distinct areas: domestic, for household needs, and communal, for the needs of the community or township as a whole. The range of tasks within each area often overlapped. While it took only one man or woman to weave a web of cloth, it took a number of women working as a team to thicken it. Also, the work of one often satisfied the needs of a number. Some members of the community were supported by a group of others because they offered some special skills. For instance, the smith was paid a certain sum for his work, the smith then being bound on his part to do all jobbing work for the group. The crofters, however, had to provide their own fuel, blow the bellows and work the fore-hammer. Thus, domestic and community work was an act of concert on behalf of the members in crofting townships and produced a pattern of life which, though far from being soft, was made the easier by the spirit of co-operation.

In many communities, individuals were associated with certain types of work. Thus, one woman might be an expert in dyeing and spinning, or in weaving; another in making butter and cheese; yet another in bread-making. As for the men in the community, their work, not so tied to satisfying domestic requirements, was performed more in small teams for ploughing, sowing, harvesting, fishing, the care of livestock, building houses and repairing dykes and fences.

From an early age, children were introduced to the subtleties of their parents' work, so that when they reached their majority they fitted into their community roles with an exactness which ensured their continuity into the future. Only in the latter decades of Victoria's reign, and through the years of Edward's, did outside influences begin to impinge with any significance on to the rhythms of community life, to introduce some

58 A spinner and her husband from Iona, *c.*1885. The spinning wheel is unusual in its elaborate ornamentation which is reminiscent of function in the bobbin-reel turnings. A wheel contemporary with Flora MacDonald (1750) has similar decoration

59 'Winning' peats in Strathspey; 1890

syncopation which was in fact the beginning of the end of the interdependence of the members of the community. Coals imported from the south (at Brora in east Sutherland they had their own coal mine) meant that the activity associated with peat-cutting was diminished in importance. Fertilisers brought by boat and rail resulted in fewer journeys to the shore for seaweed. Chemical dyes saved time in haunting the moors for flowers and plants to reduce them to the agents needed for dyeing cloth. Mills could offer ready-spun yarn to the weaver and eliminate the long and laborious work of carding and spinning. Mills of another sort could offer sacks of ready-ground meal to make the quern a nostalgic ornament outside the front door.

These importations eroded the relationships which once existed between the members of Highland communities. Work tended to be performed for a cash wage, and this in turn created a new importance for Highland towns, where shops catered for an increasing demand for all kinds of goods. The township carpenter found less demand for his services, because factory-made furniture could now be bought. The shoemaker gravitated to the town and let the countryfolk come to him, instead of him having to travel round the villages in the hinterland. Lipton's stores could offer butter and cheese. Thatched roofs gave way to corrugated iron. Domestic chores, too, became easier as the design of houses changed with the advance of science and reacted to new ideas.

However, as we see here, the rhythms of life were still those of nature, for it was to take a decade or two after the death of King Edward before the region began to ape what the rest of the country had adopted years before.

60 Fetching home peats on Skye; *c.*1890

61 Sorting staples of wool
before dyeing; Harris, c.1900

62 Washing clothes in Skye;
c.1890

63 Weaving in Harris, 1910, on an old heavy wood loom

64 Three stages in producing yarn. To the right the young lass is using wool cards (flat boards with sharp metal teeth to tease the wool fibres straight); the woman in the centre is spinning from the card rolls; to the left the woman is winding yarn from the spinning wheel into hanks. Photograph taken on Skye, *c.*1890

65 Members of a Lewis crofting family pose for a photograph with a *cas-chrom* (bent or crooked spade) and an old stone quern for grinding corn; *c.*1890

66 Grinding corn on a quern in Skye; *c.*1890

67 Making ropes from heather
stems; Outer Hebrides, c.1905

68 Butter-making at Tarrel
Farm, Easter Ross; c.1906

69 A thatcher at work repairing a roof at Poolewe, Wester Ross; *c.*1880

70 Shoemaker at Woodend, Glen Lyon, Perthshire. This craftsman is Alexander Stewart, self-educated and author of *A Highland Parish*, a minor classic, published in Glasgow in 1928, and now a scarce example of its genre; 1912

71 A pretty lass with a net basket, eastern Highlands; *c.* 1900

72 Crofters stock-taking on Barra; *c.*1890

73 Unloading coals from a 'puffer', Easter Ross; *c.*1890

74 Baiting the long lines, eastern Highlands; 1879

PEOPLE AT WORK
The Land

Land, its possession, use and its final alienation from the folk of the Highlands, has ever been an important element in the region's social and economic history. The Highlander, using simple pastoral and agrarian techniques, backed by a non-urban culture, and, moderating the effects of climatic and biotic factors, has produced an environment for living which still largely survives. The Highland 'problem' of our time has a taproot which goes deep into the past; it reached a certain degree of acuteness when the patriarchal clan system of government was finally broken after the Jacobite Rising of 1745. A new way of life had then to be found, for the land was being overtaken by external interests. The natural resources of the forests were rapidly depleted for purposes far beyond the needs of the people within the region; extensive sheep-farming replaced the former indigenous cattle industry which had made the region one of the most productive in Europe. Sheep gave way to deer as the former gradually rendered the land derelict with their method of grazing; the deer reduced the derelict land into an infertile state. Finally, the large-scale planting of non-deciduous trees made for a waste land which, though enchanting to the eye of the tourist, was tantamount to desert.

Life, however, had to be lived as best it could and the land, almost the *raison d'être* for living, worked into some small state of fertility to produce a few potatoes, feed a cow or two, or provide peat for the fires during the winter months. This it did, but not without much back-breaking persuasion on the part of folk who grew old before their time. Time and time again the potato crop failed, often followed by the loss of the grain harvest, with the result that the spectre of starvation was a regular visitor to many poor houses in the region. Little wonder, then, that feelings ran high in the early eighties of last century to such an extent that the Government of the day decided, in its doubtful wisdom, that the only solution was a visit from a military force to put down a people who, though riotous, never sought to make use of arms. In the event, the crofter was given legal status in the Crofters' Holdings (Scotland) Act of June 1886. But, given security of tenure, he was not allowed the logical extension of right to

75 Young St Kildan woman using a scythe; *c.*1890

76 Collecting seaweed for fertiliser; South Uist, *c*.1890

develop his land to bring it back into its old degree of fertility, on which Highland society had been based, and that successfully, in previous centuries.

In the illustrations, folk are busy carrying out the daily tasks upon which the continuity of life depended. Fertiliser in the coastal and maritime districts meant seaweed from the shore; though some landlords forbade the use of the weed in this way. Inland, dung and limestone were used. Agricultural implements were primitive: it required cash to buy the articles needed to do other than scratch the topsoil. The use of the *cas chrom* was widespread. This was the bent-foot plough, a special type of spade designed for use in places where the soil depth was shallow. Evolved over centuries of use, with local variations, the foot plough performed a central role in land-use activities. Other implements were just as crude. Often, small patches of land could be reaped only by the use of the *corran*, a small hand sickle. A common form of land use was the rig, a raised plateau of soil, well-fertilised with seaweed and surrounded by a deep moat or ditch. These *feannagan* or lazybeds – though they were far from being idle patches – were a common sight last century and their remains can still be seen as faint running scars around deserted clusters of houses.

Crops included the essential potato, grain such as barley and oats, and turnips.

Grazing land was carefully used, with animals given a preferential placing in terms of the damage caused to the land when feeding. Thus, one cow, an important animal, was equal to one-half horse, eight sheep, or sixteen lambs.

Harvesting was performed at the whim of the weather. A damp summer left nothing to remind the folk of its passing but wet, black stalks. A hot dry summer left potatoes as small as marbles in the ground. Deer often raided the crofters' fields and caused irreparable damage to growing crops; before 1886 this occurrence was no grounds for complaint and compensation, for crofters were merely squatters in a legal context.

In some parts of the region, there were opportunities for paid work, particularly on large estates, where wood-felling provided a source of scarce cash and also the pickings for firewood. In other areas, fishing was the alternative occupation.

77 Hard at work with the *cas chrom* – the 'bent foot' plough – and the more modern spade; Skye, *c*.1890

78 Cutting the peats for the winter's fires; *c.*1890

79 Harvesting in the Highlands; *c.*1890

80 Crofters on Eriskay islands,
Outer Hebrides, *c.*1910. Note
the home-made panniers and
the wooden pack saddle and
pad made of woven rope

81 Planting potatoes on Skye,
*c.*1890. Note the use of seaweed
placed directly in the drills

82 Highland cattle; Skye, c.1890

83 Mishap at Reelig Estate,
Kirkhill, near Inverness; *c.*1890

84 Transplanting a full-grown
tree at Reelig Estate, Kirkhill,
near Inverness; *c.*1890

85 The meal and corn mill at Reelig Estate, Kirkhill, near Inverness; *c.*1880

86 The *Maid of Harris*, a schooner pressed into fishing service; *c.*1880

PEOPLE AT WORK
The Sea

The seas surrounding the coastal areas of the Highlands and Islands began to play their part in the region's social and economic history about three centuries ago. Before then, the sea was a useful source of food when a change of diet was needed: the St Kildans relied on seabirds for their food. Or, in the case of the MacNeils of Barra, it was a route between their own island and the northern coasts of Ireland whenever their larders or purses were in need of replenishment. On the Uists the daily casting of seaweed was gathered to make kelp. For the islands of the Hebrides, the seas often acted to both isolate and insulate their communities from influences which would have otherwise rapidly diluted their hard-won culture and lifestyle.

It was not until the seventeenth century that the fishing potential in Highland waters was realised. Three burghs (Campbeltown, Fort William and Stornoway) were erected for the accommodation of fishermen and the promotion of the fishing trade – only one instance in a long stream of 'encouragements' which failed to succeed, mainly because the needs of the fishermen and their growing industry were looked after and influenced by outsiders. The history of the Scottish fishing industry during the eighteenth century, and its relations with the State, is a record of constant effort to neutralise the handicap of the heavy salt duty which was attended by a Sargasso sea of rules and regulations that smothered any initiative on the part of the fishermen.

When, in 1830, the Salt Duty Act was repealed, and an inefficient barrel-bounty system abolished, the industry was able to put itself on a stable and self-supporting basis. By the time Queen Victoria had been on the throne a decade or so, the Scottish fishing industry was poised for nearly six decades of boom activity. The early years of Victoria's reign also saw the state entering into the industry's affairs with some purpose but with the same characteristic bureaucratic bungling as in earlier centuries. Through the 1839 Fishery Convention, a bureaucrats' paradise was produced, with a maze of regulations. In 1843 an Act was passed which was to be described as 'an extremely defective piece of legislation'. So it went on until the Sea Fisheries Act of 1868 removed a multitude of obscurities and the industry was allowed to get on with expansion. The middle years of the nineteenth century saw the introduction of trawling; later, the use of mechanical means for propulsion increased and the dependence on sail became the exception rather than the rule.

The first steam trawler appeared off Golspie, Sutherland, in 1879, to signal yet another change in the industry, one which, in particular, left many Highland communities, with their economies based on the more traditional methods of catching and sailing, at a great disadvantage. For the most part, Highland fishermen were employees rather than employers, working for a wage (often supplemented by a goodly measure of tobacco and whisky at the end of the season). In many places, the invidious 'truck' system operated, in which goods and food were given on credit until debts were settled at the end of the season. Frequently, however, the final 'settlement' absorbed all of a fisherman's cash and forced him deeper into the debt of the shop-owner who, more often than not, was the principal shareholder in the boat employing the fisherman.

Inevitably, in an effort to increase the family income, women entered the industry to become an important work force; they followed the herring as the shoals moved round the coasts of the British Isles. The women were gutters and could earn in one season enough to keep a whole family together for a year. By about 1890 it was estimated that about three-quarters of the whole population of the western Highlands and Islands were engaged in fishing.

Fishing was not without its loss of life; the history of many coastal communities is filled with the news of ships lost at sea, menfolk drowned, and wreckings, often within the sight and sound of those waiting helplessly on a shoreline as a boat tried to clear a harbour bar or make the lee of a cliff.

This is the background to the photographs in this section. However romantic, picturesque and innocent the views might be, they belie the hard work and grinding toil which they represent.

The final years of King Edward's reign saw the beginning of the decline in the role of the sea in the Highland economy, and ushered in the onset of a period of depression that was to last for nearly five decades. As the patterns of life changed, ships brought goods from far-off places. Ships also carried away many thousands of Highlanders to America, New Zealand, Australia and Canada, as emigrants escaping from an oppressive way of life which offered nothing but uncertainty and continual poverty. However, the period covered in these pictures show the folk participating in the comparative prosperity of the later years of Victoria's reign, and the ships they sailed to gain their share of the riches of the sea.

87   Fishing in the calm waters of Loch Maree, an inland water in Wester Ross; c.1890

88 The *Main*, registered at Stornoway, Lewis. This type of fishing vessel was known as a 'Zulu', because it appeared at the time when the South African war had just been concluded. The boats carried enormous sails, like great brown pyramids, 70 feet above water level. Their heyday was during the 1890s

89 Cutting seaweed; Skye, *c.*1880

90 Fishing boats at Castlebay, Barra. Note the new use for an unwanted boat in the foreground. In the islands where materials were hard to come by, everything possible was 're-cycled'; *c.*1885

91 Wick Harbour, Caithness, at the height of the herring season, *c.*1885

92 On the pier at Stornoway
Harbour; *c.*1890

93 A pause from work to pose for the photographer, *c*.1890. Herring gutters at Ullapool, Wester Ross

94 Herring gutters getting their arms and backs into it at Wick Harbour, Caithness, *c*.1885

95   Dividing the catch of fulmars; St Kilda, *c*.1886

96   St Kilda islanders bring home their catch of fulmars; *c*.1886

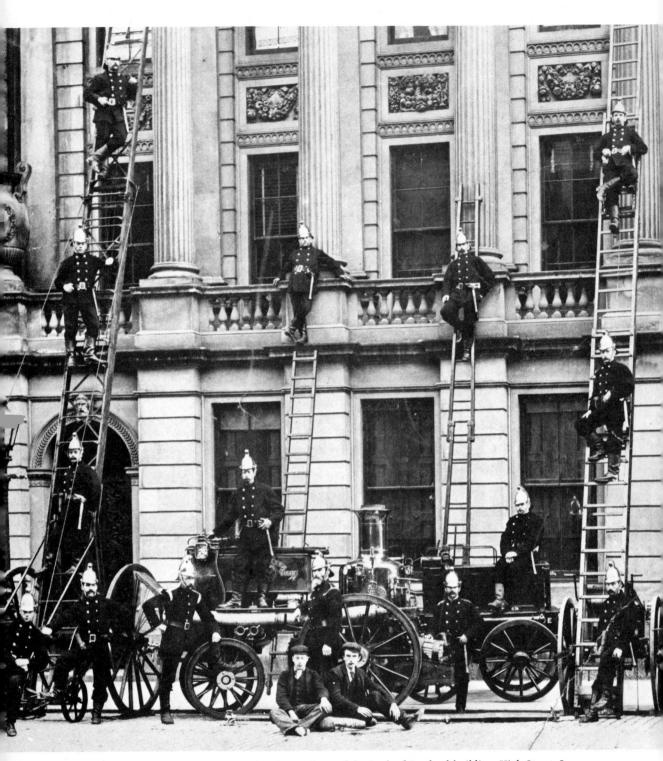

97 Inverness Fire Brigade, 1900, in front of the Bank of Scotland building, High Street, Inverness

EVENTS AND OCCASIONS

Although the Highlands and Islands tended to be on the outer periphery of the wide world located somewhat to the south and east, the region was by no means a dull place to live in. The variety of 'happenings' is seen in the photographs in this section. Some of them are not without their tragic tale: eviction from one's home was still common, despite the existence of the Crofters Act of 1886. Generally, however, events and occasions were unusual enough to talk about over the warmth of a peat fire in the late winter months.

It might be a new-fangled factory at Foyers, on the shores of Loch Ness, to produce a new metal called aluminium, a child of science less than 50 years old. The coming of the trains to Fort William, bringing the world and his wife to the hills of Lochaber was an event to be long remembered. That a Queen should reign continuously for 60 years was something that needed a high bonfire on Barra. The arrival of the motor car at John O'Groats was a day to be remembered, and we, seven decades later, are thankful that a photographer thought the occasion sufficiently important to record it through the eye of his camera.

Nor was that the end of the world's wonders. A flying-machine arrived at the Strathpeffer Games in Ross-shire in 1912, the first of many such offerings from the plate of both scientists and engineer. But it was not all drawing-board stuff. The folk of Tain had reason to resort to the quasi-magical tricks or gifts of a water-diviner, from far-off Edinburgh, to discover a new source of fresh water.

Other events touched community life: fairs, market days, the factor's reckoning for rent dues, and attendance, half-yearly, at the outdoor communions for those congregations still without a church after the Disruption of 1843. A touch of class could be added at times as when the local Fire Brigade decided to commemorate the end of one century and the beginning of another by posing for a photograph outside an imposing and certainly photogenic building in Inverness High Street.

98   The building of the new
aluminium reduction works at
Foyers, on Loch Ness side,
Inverness-shire, being inspected
by a group including Lord and
Lady Kelvin; 1895

99   Lord Allinger cutting the
first sod for the West Highland
Railway in 1888

100 The arrival at Fort William of the first train of the West Highland Railway, 1894

101 Motor car versus wheelbarrow. The driver is Hubert Egerton, a celebrated pioneer of motoring. The location is John O' Groats. The car is a Werner of the type just before 1901

102 A welcome to Hubert Egerton, motoring pioneer, on his arrival at John O' Groats on a converted bicycle driven by a petrol engine.

103 The tragic fire on T.S.M.V. *Scout* at Kinlochleven, 19 August 1913

104 The first aeroplane flight over the Highlands, piloted by B. C. Hucks. At the Strathpeffer Games, 24 August, 1912. The machine is the Daily Mail *Firefly*

First aeroplane flight in the Highlands. Mr B.C. Hucks at Strathpeffer Games. August ? with the Daily Mail "Firefly" no1. "Getting ready to start."

105 Lochaber Highland Gathering, Fort William, September 1890

106 Success! Water at Tain, Easter Ross. This bore was drilled after water was indicated by James Henderson, a water diviner from Edinburgh; *c.*1890

107 The Factor's reckoning, North Uist, 1895

108 Eviction for not paying the rent; Lochmaddy, North Uist, 1895. One of the inhabitants of the cottage, Kate MacDiarmid, who was evicted, died just before these photographs were discovered

109   Outdoor Communion for Gaelic speakers, near Migdale, Sutherlandshire; *c*.1880

110   The sailing ship *Regent* at the old pier at Foyers, on Loch Ness, *c.*1895

GETTING ABOUT

It was not until the dawning of the nineteenth century that communications in the Highlands and Islands began to emerge from a primitive state. Before then, General Wade's engineered roads and bridges, supplemented by the roads used by cattle drovers, were the only routes of any importance. Folk tended to travel along well-worn tracks. Lacking such refinements as coaches, they used shanks's pony to great effect and could travel long distances quickly with little thought but that of getting to their destination safely. As a result, Highland communities tended to be tight-knit and isolated. But the potential of the region was being realised by both politician and speculator, who set about making more areas accessible to development and therefore traffic. In the west, 'destitution roads' were constructed after the failures of the potato crops in 1846 and 1847. These roads were built by starving cottars who were, more often than not, paid in kind: meal and other foodstuffs rather than in cash. The road from Braemore to Aultbea in Wester Ross is still called 'Destitution Road', so long do these events survive in residual folk memory.

These roads were never up to the standards of some of the older turnpike roads which had been introduced by Statute into Scotland from 1750 onwards, under the 1750 Turnpike Act. Many Ministers complained about the state of the roads in their parishes when they sent in their contributions to the New Statistical Account (1840). Nevertheless, what roads there were made for easier travel, and coaches were to become commonplace in time.

Road construction was far from being an easy task, from the viewpoint of both labourer and engineer. The road to Applecross, in Wester Ross, featured in this section of photographs, presented a problem solved only by hairpin bends to accommodate the steep gradients involved. By the time the Edwardian era ended, the region was fairly accessible, even though a journey to remote places was still something of the nature of a safari.

Water transport was common between islands, and between the mainland and off-shore islands. Small ferries, of long-standing operation and reputation, were always kept busy. The two Highland canals, the Crinan and the Caledonian, were conceived on the right lines, but were doomed to be permanent loss-makers. Even so, they made it possible to sail direct from Glasgow to Inverness and thence northwards to the islands of Orkney and Shetland, by-passing turbulent seas.

Possibly the railway contributed more to opening up the mainland Highlands than any other form of transport. The Highland Railway Company and the West Highland Railway Company, with thoughts of big profits, raised capital and began railway cuttings. In 1865 the former concern opened up lines between Perth and Inverness, Inverness and Ross-shire, and lines eastwards to Aberdeen. Skye could be reached by rail car by 1870, as could Sutherland and Caithness. By 1886, the mineral waters of the Strathpeffer Spa in Ross-shire could be tasted after a train journey; and Fort William saw the first sod being cut by Lord Allinger in 1888. In 1903 the extension of the Sutherland Railway to Wick and Lybster was completed. Fares were delightfully cheap: for instance, one could travel the quarter-mile between Culrain and Invershin, in Sutherland, for one halfpenny.

The appearance of the motor car towards the end of Queen Victoria's reign heralded yet another phase in the opening up of the region. Though mechanical curiosities at first, the folk of the Highlands were not slow to replace their horse-, dog-, and pony-drawn carts with carriages driven by steam and petrol engines; many previously quiet roads resounded to the chugging of motors to startle deer, sheep and cattle, if not a few older-generation natives. The advent of the motor car meant, too, that tourists could make their own way to visit such places as John O'Groats, previously known only as names on the map. These early years often became a matter of 'firsts' of Speke and Burton proportions: the first to reach the far north, the farthest west, or the first to cross a ferry at Kyle, Bona, Corran and Ballachulish. Typically, a number of vehicles in the photographs in this section are from places far distant from the Highlands.

The production of noise to disturb an otherwise peaceful countryside was not the monopoly of the motor car. The aeroplane provided the rare opportunity for viewing the Highlands as no other eyes, save those of the soaring golden eagle, had seen them before; and, with the aeroplane other wonders were being created to bring the Highlands and Islands into a contemporary setting. Never again would the region find itself on the receiving end of stale world-wide news, or its womenfolk be some

111 Always time for a chat in Glen Lyon, Perthshire, c.1900

112 A family outing, 1900

decades behind the fashions of London, Paris and New York.

Of course, the simpler forms of transport were still looked on as being good enough and, indeed, were more personal. One could always stop a bicycle, pony-and-trap, or dog cart, for a chat with a passing friend or stranger.

While the trains were building up their own clientele, the ships of the west coast and on the canals were in their heyday. Many of their names were household words as they plied the waters over decades, carrying fathers and sons from coast to coast and taking the world's goods to humble homes. But sail gave way to steam, steam was superseded by diesel engines; and ships were to be designed on functional lines rather than to give beauty and pleasure to the eye.

113 Everyone keeps still except the horses; in the Pass of Melfort, Argyll, *c.*1900

114 Crossing the old Inverness Bridge in 1885

115 A full load, *c*.1910

116 A rough road in the West Highlands, *c.* 1895. The road, Bealach nam Bo (Pass of the Cattle), climbs from sea level to 2000 feet in six miles. This is the road to the Applecross community. The car registration is AF 1, a far-travelled visitor from Cornwall

117   Tain Cycling Club in 1889, with penny-farthing bicycles and a tricycle (the latter weighed 3 cwts); 1889

118   A train of the Highland
Railway at Auchterneed, near
Dingwall, during the great
snowstorm of December 1906

119   The station at Kyle of Lochalsh, *c.*1900

120 Out with the shovels in a snow-lock in the winter of 1895

121　The paddle-steamer *Gondolier* going through the locks at Fort Augustus on the Caledonian Canal, *c*.1800. Built in 1866, she was in service for over 70 years until 1939, when her hull was towed to Scapa Flow for sinking to block a passage

122　On the Crinan Canal, with the S.S. *Linnet* in the centre, *c*.1885

123   At Corpach on the Caledonian Canal, *c*.1880; Ben Nevis behind

124 The S.S. *Lochiel*, berthed at Tarbert, Argyll, 1880. Built in 1878, she sailed as far north as Inverness. In 1884 she was fitted out for a three-month cruise in the neighbourhood of Skye, with a gunboat in attendance, to help suppress the crofters' riots expected to result from the then recently initiated legislation introduced by the London Land Reform Association. She was broken up after she ran aground at Portree, Skye, in 1907

125 The first car to cross the Ballachulish ferry, 1 May 1906. The car registration is Southport

126 The P.S. *Grenadier* at the jetty off Iona, *c.*1895. She was launched in 1885 and was burnt out when a serious fire occurred one night in 1927 when lying alongside the North Pier at Oban. Some of her crew lost their lives

SPORT AND PLEASURE

By the late Victorian years, when it came to be realised that the savage clearance of people from the Highlands to make way for sheep had been an act of social and economic folly, in that the land had become derelict, landowners looked to other methods to make their vast acres pay. The easiest was to offer their estates to shooting and fishing tenants; so it was that the Victorian era saw the advent of the Highland sporting estate. But this was available only to the rich; lesser mortals had to make do with simpler, though parallel pleasures. Some of these are featured in this section. They indicate that life in the region had a silver lining to it.

The tourist, too, was beginning to find out the delights of the region, aided and abetted by easier travel to places hitherto thought as inaccessible as Timbuctoo or Siberia. They came in droves to seek out whatever the region had to offer. They viewed with delight the tall, dignified standing stones at Callanish, Lewis, rivals to both Stonehenge and Carnac in Brittany. They looked askance at the poor homes and their inhabitants, at the out-moded dress, and tried to understand the Gaelic-coloured English in which the natives conversed.

More than likely, one of the 'musts' on their list of places to visit was Ben Nevis, the highest mountain in Britain, to be literally on top of the Highland world. Of particular interest was the Ben Nevis Observatory. It was built in 1883 as a Meterological Observatory with publicly-subscribed funds and was managed by the Scottish Meterological Society and representatives of the Royal Societies of Edinburgh and London. Hourly observations were maintained for 21 years and sent by telegraph via Fort William to meterological services throughout Europe. The Brocken Spectre was seen here on cloud in the Great Corrie by G. T. R. Wilson in 1894, an event which led him to researches which culminated in the Wilson Cloud Chamber for which he was to be awarded the Nobel Prize.

The materials for the building had to be taken to the summit on horseback. At a height of 4406 feet above sea level, the Observatory made significant contributions to the art and science of weather forecasting. An attraction to visitors' facilities was a

127 Stalking deer, the privilege of the upper classes in the Highlands; Inverewe, c.1890

small hotel and a refreshments room. The Ben was extremely popular: who indeed could follow a visit to the summit by anything more exciting?

128 Swan-shooting on North Uist; c.1895

129   A mixed bag from a shoot by members of Tain Gun Club, Easter Ross; *c*.1890

130   Posing for the photographer after a good shoot; *c*.1900

131   In the new golf course at Culcabock, Inverness; 1885

132 The first of many to come. A tourist poses beside the Standing Stones at Callanish, Lewis; *c.*1890

133   Inside the Ben Nevis Observatory, 1885

134 A moment of relaxation after a hard day's work, but not for the fingers of the fisher girls busy with their knitting; 1910

INDUSTRY

Although the Highlands of Scotland escaped the social evils of the Industrial Revolution, industry was no stranger to the region. In 1607 a large ironworks was established at Letterewe, beside Loch Maree in Ross-shire. Sir Robert Gordon commented on the abundance of iron ore in Sutherland 'of which the inhabitants make good iron'. The furnace site at Letterewe is the earliest historic ironwork in Scotland. Slate-quarrying, timber operations, charcoal-burning and ship-building were also well established in the Highlands by the time Queen Victoria came to the throne. But these were in the nature of local pockets of industry: their impact on the overall Highland scene was minimal. They were, however, important social sheet-anchors, for they offered employment to those who were unable to become tenants or obtain some land to work.

One example of the introduction of large-scale operations of an industrial nature was the York Buildings Company, of London, which took a lease of Abernethy pine forest. The Company started work by building sawmills and an iron foundry and, with 125 work horses, dragged the trees to the banks of the river Spey. The logs were then floated downstream. Perhaps surprisingly, the works were managed by Aaron Hill, the poet, playwright, traveller and erstwhile manager of Drury Lane Theatre. Later, some of the workers from Speyside were transferred to another of the Company's operations: the lead mines at Strontian, in the Ardnamurchan peninsula.

The second quarter of the eighteenth century was an important period in the establishment of the Scottish iron industry: several works were then started in the Highlands. The Bonawe furnace was in existence by 1711; the Invergarry furnace was in use by 1730, while the Abernethy furnace was established in Strathspey to reduce haematite brought nearly 20 miles by packhorse. The ironmasters who selected the site at Invergarry in 1727 faced the tremendous problems of transporting ore from a wharf at Corpach, near Fort William, overland to Loch Lochy, thence by boat and overland again to Invergarry. The furnace lasted for less than seven years. The furnace at Bonawe saw a second lease of life when it was re-erected in the 1870s at Ulverston by the company operating the last two charcoal furnaces in Britain.

Textiles, too, created industrial operations, though it was generally 'cottage' in nature, in that spinning and weaving were carried out in the homes of the folk. Coarse woollen cloths and linen were exported in large quantities; but the introduction of American cotton products spelled anathema to the Highland operations.

One of the principal sources of income in the years of the first half of the nineteenth century was kelp. So important was this industry that it helped to maintain the surplus population on the coastal fringes of the west of Scotland; its eventual decline, together with the periodic famines, reduced the basis of life to very low levels and the failure of the potato harvests in the 1840s made the middle of the nineteenth century the nadir of crofting life. The industry continued sporadically in the Inner and Outer Hebrides, chiefly in the Uists, until the turn of the twentieth century when it provided a small pocket of employment to crofters in desperate straits.

Industry in the modern sense arrived in the Highlands during the last years of Victoria's reign. The region's large reserves of water power were essential to the cheap production of aluminium. The British Aluminium Company, to which Lord Kelvin was the first technical adviser, began operations in 1896 at the Falls of Foyers on the eastern shore of Loch Ness, with a 5000-horsepower hydro-electric plant. Although the plant produced one-tenth of the world's supply of aluminium of 2000 tons per annum, its capacity was not fully utilised. By 1904 the world production of aluminium had risen to 9000 tons, and to increase output the Company began new operations at Kinloch-leven, using power from the Blackwater Reservoir. By 1909 the Company was producing 10,000 tons of aluminium, or about one-third of the world production. Thus, the Highlands entered the world of big industry.

But another industry, also destined to become international in its operations, was quietly developing from its smuggling origins. This was the production of whisky. An Act of Parliament of 1823 was the 'breakthrough' following which it became possible to sell whisky openly. The result was that those who had been producing spirits in defiance of the law were encouraged to come forward with the skills they had preserved as outlaws and practised them with the blessing of the law. Right through the years of the nineteenth century successive Acts of Parliament were passed to improve and regulate the distilling of whisky in Scotland and particularly in the Highlands. Slowly moonshine became a spirit of the daylight and provided important employment facilities in a region otherwise deprived of these.

Occasionally a little bit of excitement occurred. The Kildonan Gold Rush was an example. Alluvial gold was discovered in the Straths of Kildonan in Sutherland in 1868 and hundreds of prospectors headed north to participate in the Highland Klondyke. But, after months of panning proved fruitless for many, they left. The metal was as elusive as the treasure at the end of the rainbow.

Perhaps the Kildonan gold rush of last century symbolises the Highlands and Islands of Scotland, in that the real treasures of the region are not to be found in material things, but rather in the intangibles which abound in such a magnificent country which offers so many challenges to both body and spirit.

135 Inside a Speyside distillery, *c*.1910

136 Delivering barley to a distillery in the eastern Highlands, *c.*1877

137 Workmen constructing the first modern factory in the Highlands: the aluminium reduction works at Foyers, Inverness-shire; 1896

138　Some of the workmen who helped to build the lighthouse on Eilean Mor, one of the Flannan Isles
group of Atlantic outliers off the coast of Lewis; 1895